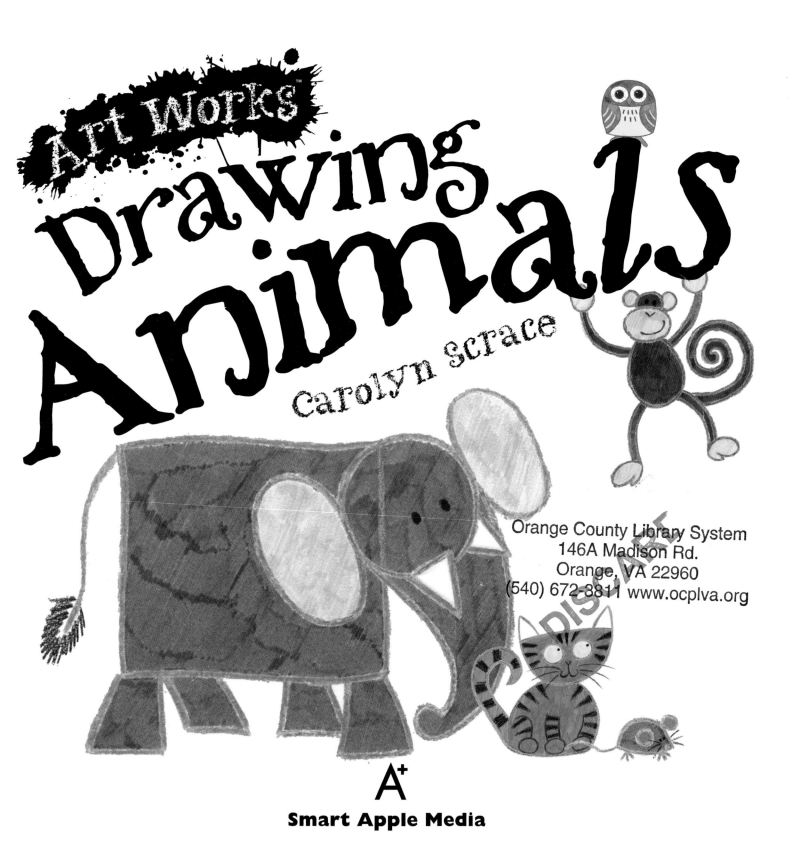

Art Works™

Drawing Animals

Carolyn Scrace

A+

Smart Apple Media

Author:
Carolyn Scrace graduated from Brighton
College of Art, England, after studying design
and illustration. Since then she has worked in
animation, advertising, and children's
publishing. She has a special interest in natural
history and has written many books on the
subject, including *Lion Journal* and *Gorilla Journal*
in the *Animal Journal* series.

How to use this book:

Follow the easy, numbered instructions.
Simple step-by-step stages enable
budding young artists to create their
own amazing drawings.

What you will need:

1. Paper to draw on.
2. Wax crayons for drawing.
3. Felt-tip pens to color in
   your drawings.

Published by Smart Apple Media,
an imprint of Black Rabbit Books
P.O. Box 3263, Mankato, Minnesota 56002
www.blackrabbitbooks.com

Published by arrangement with
The Salariya Book Company Ltd

Cataloging-in-Publication Data is available
from the Library of Congress

Printed in the United States
At Corporate Graphics,
North Mankato, Minnesota

9 8 7 6 5 4

ISBN: 978-1-62588-343-8

Contents

A Cat

1 A cat needs a head,

2 ...a body,

3 ...two ears,

4 ...a tail,

5 ...and big, round, green eyes!

6 Now draw his legs and paws.

4

Finish drawing
in the cat's eyes.
Then crayon in
some stripes.

Add a nose,
mouth, and
whiskers.

Color in with
felt-tip pens.

5

An Owl

1 An owl needs a body,

2 ...a head,

3 ...big round eyes,

4 ...two wings,

5 ...a beak, and two feet!

6 Now draw in the owl's feathers.

Color in with
felt-tip pens.

7

A Zebra

1 A zebra needs a body,

2 ...a neck and head,

3 ...two front legs,

4 ...two back legs,

Mane

5 ...two ears, and a tail!

6 Now crayon in his eyes, nose, mane, and the tip of his tail.

8

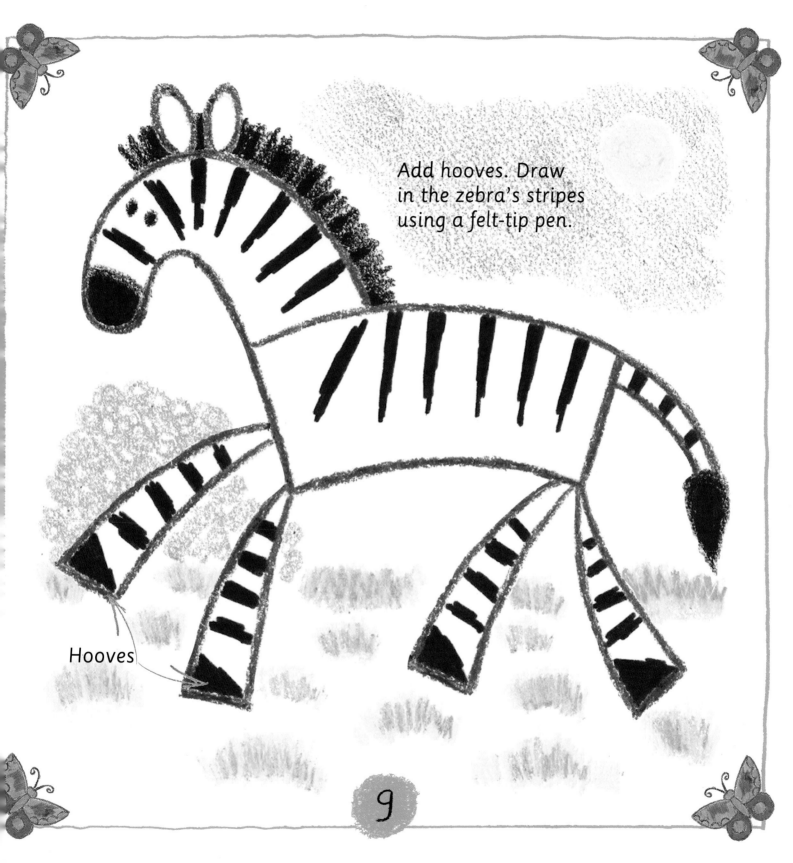

Add hooves. Draw
in the zebra's stripes
using a felt-tip pen.

Hooves

A Ladybug

1 A ladybug needs a body,

2 ...a head,

3 ...legs,

4 ...an eye,

5 ...and spots!

6 Now color in her head, spots, and legs with felt-tip pens.

Draw in the ladybug's
eye and antennae.

Antennae

Color in with
felt-tip pens.

11

A Whale

1 A whale needs a body,

2 ...a tail,

3 ...a flipper,

Blowhole

4 ...and an eye, mouth, and blowhole!

Draw in the whale's eye and curvy lines for her waterspout.

Waterspout

Color in with felt-tip pens.

13

An Elephant

1 An elephant needs a body,

2 ...a head,

3 ...a trunk,

4 ...two big ears,

5 ...four legs,

6 ...a tail, and tusks!

Color in with
felt-tip pens.

Draw in the elephant's
eyes and finish her tail.

15

A Lion

1 A lion needs a head,

2 ...a body,

3 ...four legs,

4 ...two ears, and a tail!

Mane

Draw in the lion's face and his beautiful big mane.

Color in with felt-tip pens.

17

A Panda

1 A panda needs a head,

2 ...a body,

3 ...two arms,

4 ...and two legs!

5 Now draw in the panda's markings,

6 ...and his ears and eyes.

Draw in the panda's
nose and mouth,
and finish his eyes.

Color in with
felt-tip pens.

A Dog

1 A dog needs a head,

2 ...a body,

3 ...four legs,

4 ...a collar, a tail,

5 ...a nose, and ears!

6 Crayon in his body.
Leave some white patches.

20

Draw in the dog's eyes, mouth, and whiskers.

Add curvy lines to make him wag his tail!

Color in with *felt-tip pens*.

A Frog

1 A frog needs a head,

2 ...a body,

3 ...two legs,

4 ...two feet,

5 ...two arms, two hands,

6 ...great big eyes, and spots!

Draw in the frog's eyes, nose, and mouth.

Color in with felt-tip pens.

23

A Giraffe

1 A giraffe needs a body,

2 ...a long neck,

3 ...four legs,

4 ...a head, a tail,

5 ...ears, and horns!

6 Draw a square pattern on her neck and body.

24

Draw in the giraffe's
eyes, nose,
and mouth.

Color in with
felt-tip pens.

25

A Fox

1 A fox needs a head,

2 ...a body,

3 ...a neck,

4 ...four legs,

5 ...a big bushy tail,

6 ...and two ears! Add an eye.

Draw in the fox's nose,
mouth, and whiskers,
and finish his eyes.

Draw in his neck,
chest, and tail markings.

Color in with
felt-tip pens.

27

A Crocodile

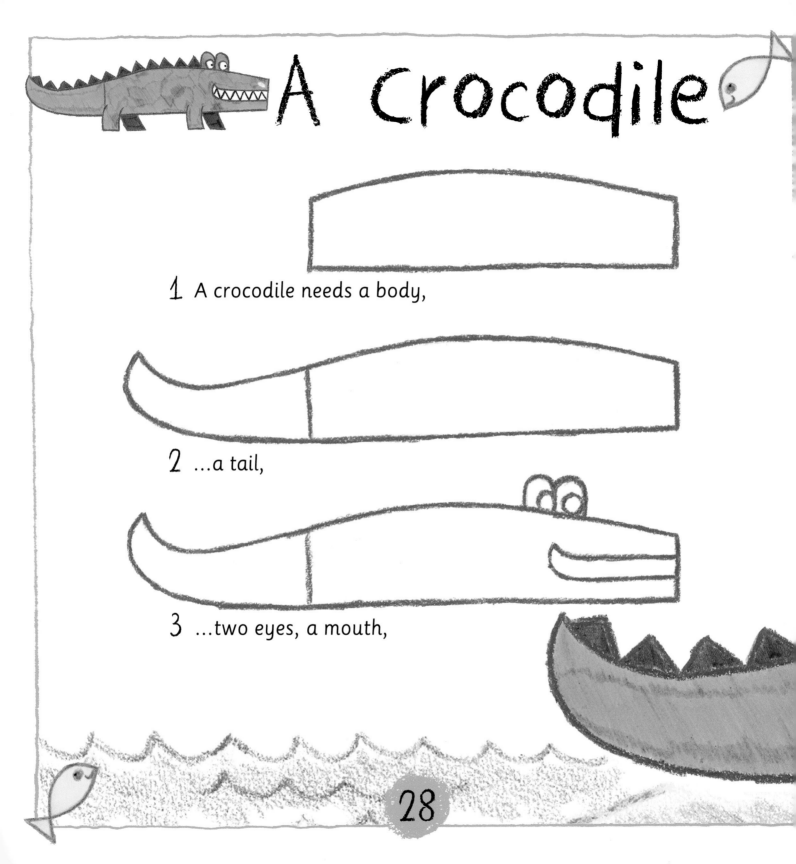

1 A crocodile needs a body,

2 ...a tail,

3 ...two eyes, a mouth,

28

4 ...and four stumpy legs!

5 Now add a zigzag line to
the top of the crocodile's body.

Draw in his sharp
teeth and
finish his eyes.

Color in with
felt-tip pens.

A Monkey

1 A monkey needs a head,

2 ...a body,

3 ...two arms and two legs,

4 ...two hands and two feet,

5 ...two big ears,

6 ...and a long, curly tail!

30

Draw in the monkey's
eyes, nose, and mouth.

Color in with
felt-tip pens.

31

Glossary

Antennae   an insect's feelers.

Blowhole   what a whale breathes through.

Hooves   the hard, lower parts of some animals' feet.

Mane   long hair along the neck or around the head of some animals.

Markings   different colored patches on an animal.

Trunk   an elephant's nose, used to breathe, suck up water, and to pick up food.

Tusk   a long, strong, pointed tooth, used to get food.

Waterspout   a spout of water formed when a whale breathes out.

Index